The Ethics of Human Development

— *Quick Guide* —

David Thomas, PhD

Copyright © 2025, D. Thomas

Copyright © 2025 by David Thomas, PhD

All rights reserved. No part of this publication may be reproduced, stored in a retrieval system, or transmitted, in any form or by any means, electronic, mechanical, photocopying, recording, or otherwise, without the prior written permission of the author.

Distributed by Fifty-Six Street Press

Cover art: Paula Ziegman

Cover design: David Thomas

This book is one of several materials that make up the *Ethics of Human Development Training Program*. For more information on this program, go to davidthomasphe.com or contact David Thomas, PhD: dtec@cox.net

To The Reader: The purpose of this small book is to provide the reader with ready access to the ethics of human development.

The ethics are presented without explanation. For those seeing the ethics for the first time, the quotes accompanying the ethics may help explain them.

For the purposes of this book, it is enough to say that the ethics of human development offer an elaborated work ethic, one that serves the development of both the individual who embraces it and the organization(s) of which he or she is a part.

Lest there be any confusion, the ethics of human development are meant to apply to and serve all members of the organization, from front line worker to executive director or CEO.

> *"There is no such thing as business ethics, only people ethics. ...the 'code' must be within every employee."*
>
> James A. Autry
> *Love and Profit*

Ethic 1

The Organizational Ethic

It is ethical to serve, refine, and advance the organization[1] you have chosen to join. It is unethical to harm it.

[1]For "organization" read: business, corporation, agency, institution, team, etc., as appropriate.

From this ethic, several corollaries follow:

Ethic 1 Corollaries:

1) *It is ethical to learn everything you can about the organization of which you are a part, including its overall purpose; the vision that guides it; its rules, practices, and procedures; its parts and how they are connected; its history and status.* It is unethical to remain organizationally ignorant.

2) *It is ethical to learn about the needs of those served by your organization (i.e., who they are and what they value), and it is also ethical to learn about the needs of those within the organization served by your division or part.* It is unethical to remain ignorant of the needs of those you serve, whether they are customers, consumers, clients, students, patients or fellow employees.

3) *It is ethical to perform your role (i.e., your job or duty) accurately, efficiently, and pleasantly.* It is unethical not to do your job to the best of your ability.

4) *It is ethical to perform your role (i.e., your job or duty) in a fashion that does not add to the work, hardship, or distraction of others unnecessarily.* It is unethical to make work unnecessarily harder for others.

5) *It is ethical to speak fairly and honestly of organizational members; to say about them what you are willing to say to them. The same applies to the organization as a whole.* It is unethical to engage in malicious gossip, ridicule, or derisive humor.

6) *It is ethical to follow the rules, practices, and procedures of the organization.* It is unethical to willfully and knowingly violate the rules, practices, and procedures of the organization or to remain ignorant of them.

NOTE: At the same time, it is naive to think that rules are never to be broken. Therefore, it is ethical to make exceptions to rules, practices, and procedures when such exceptions serve or do not harm the organization. Further, it is ethical to share the reasoning behind these exceptions so that this reasoning can be examined and refined and so that others in the organization can sooner recognize when and where exceptions are appropriate. It is ethical to help others in the organization acquire the discernment that allows them to make exceptions to rules, practices, and procedures when such exceptions serve or do not harm the organization.

7) *It is ethical to seek the correction, modification, and/or revision of rules, practices, and procedures that are inconsistent with the overall purpose and stated values of the organization.* It is unethical to accept without seeking to correct organizational practices that harm the ability of the organization to accomplish its purpose.

8) *It is ethical to create organizational improvements. These improvements may be in the form of or result in increased revenue, decreased costs, improved services, or an enhanced organizational culture.* But whatever the form or result, it is unethical not to help the organization evolve.

9) *It is ethical to protect and defend the organization against destructive influences such as outside forces or internal decision-making practices that lead to fraud, libel, or abuse.* It is unethical to remain silent in the face of perceived threats to the organization's survival.

10) *It is ethical to leave an organization whose purpose and values conflict with your own.* It is unethical to remain in an organization that requires you to violate your values or personal code of ethics.

> "Work exists for the refinement of character."
>
> E. F. Schumacher
> Economist

Ethic 2

The Open Mindedness Ethic

It is ethical to be open to the possibility that your view is incomplete, capable of expansion and improvement. It is unethical to ignore information that could allow you and/or your organization to grow.

> *"To become aware of what is happening, I must pay attention with an open mind. I must set aside my personal prejudices or bias. Prejudiced people see only what fits those prejudices."*
>
> John Heider
> *The Tao of Leadership*

Ethic 3

The Deliberate Action Ethic

It is ethical to choose consciously and execute deliberately specific actions that you believe represent the best of your discernible options. When the time to act has come, it is unethical not to do something.

(NOTE: Ethic 3 is the companion ethic to Ethic 2; each without the other is incomplete.)

> *"The first thing to do in life is to do with purpose what one proposes to do."*
>
> Pablo Casals
> Cellist

> *"I just have to make sure I mean every note."*
>
> Pharoah Sanders
> Saxophonist

Ethic 4

The Feedback Ethic

It is ethical to request, encourage, and deliver feedback. It is unethical to ignore or discourage feedback.

Ethic 4 Corollaries:

1) It is ethical to request and encourage feedback on your performance, product(s), and materials from individuals with whom you interact and/or who, in one way or another, receive your services whether they are inside or outside the organization. It is unethical to ignore or discourage feedback.

2) It is ethical to offer feedback to those from whom you or your organization receives services. It is ethical to acknowledge outstanding performance, just as it is ethical to provide feedback to those whose performance or service threatens the optimal performance of you or your organization. In both cases, it may be unethical not to do so.

3) It is ethical to deliver feedback sensitively and to accept it graciously. It is unethical to diminish the person to whom you are giving feedback or to punish the person from whom you are receiving it.

> *"No system can operate humanely without feedback."*
>
> Philip Slater
> *Earth Walk*

Ethic 5

The Truth-Telling Ethic

It is ethical to tell the truth, to be honest. It is unethical to lie. Lying creates misinformation, confusion, and distrust.

Restatement of Ethic 5:

It is ethical to tell the truth, to be honest. Truth telling promotes clarity and allows you to match resources with greater precision to the demands of the moment. It is unethical to lie. Lying creates misinformation, confusion, and distrust, threatening your ability (and the organization's ability) to survive, adapt, and prosper.

Only if the individual cannot utilize the truth constructively for personal growth are we justified in withholding it. And making such a judgment requires a discernment of an exalted degree… This was M. Scott Peck's point in his book, *The Road Less Traveled*, and having made this point he cautions, *"…in assessing the capacity of another to utilize the truth for personal/spiritual growth, it should be borne in mind that our tendency is generally to underestimate rather than overestimate this capacity."*

Ethic 6

The Pain-Directed Ethic

It is ethical to work first on the issue causing the organization (or your part of it) the most pain; and when that has been resolved or its resolution underway, to work on the next most painful issue, and so on. It is unethical to ignore painful issues.

Restatement of Ethic 6:

It is ethical in ongoing personal and organizational development to work first on the issue causing the most pain, and then to work on the next most painful issue, and so on, in this way creating improvements in the sequence most likely to ensure not only survival but also health and wellbeing. It is unethical to ignore painful issues. By ignoring painful issues, we allow them to compound, threatening all the more the ability of the person or organization to accomplish his or its purpose.

" . . . Everything we shut our eyes to, everything we run away from, everything we deny, denigrate or despise, serves to defeat us in the end."
                        Henry Miller
                        20th-century American writer

Ethic 7

The Free Choice Ethic

It is ethical to assume that you are choosing to do all that you do, that you come to your tasks by choice, that you are involved voluntarily. It is unethical to assume, unless extreme circumstances prevail, that you are being made or forced to do anything.

Restatement of Ethic 7:

It is ethical to assume that you are freely choosing to do all that you do within the context of your organization, that you come to every task by choice having concluded for yourself that the task is consistent with your values and in service to the organization's mission. It is unethical to assume that within the context of the organization—the organization you have chosen to join and from which you are free to exit—that you are being made or forced to do anything.

Which team is more likely to succeed: the team comprised of volunteers or the team comprised of individuals behaving as if they are required to participate?

Bad Faith -- *"pretending things are mandatory when they are in fact voluntary."*

> Jean Paul Sartre
> 20th-century French philosopher

Ethic 8

The Conscious Mistakes Ethic

It is ethical to eliminate conscious mistakes. It is unethical to engage in them.

Restatement of Ethic 8:

It is ethical to reduce and eliminate conscious mistakes. It is unethical to know that what you are about to do is wrong and to do it anyway.

> "This is what ordinary people mean when they say that, although men may differ as to what things are right or wrong, no one ever thinks that it is right to do wrong or wrong to do right."
>
> Wilbur Marshall Urban
> 20th-century philosopher

> "It is by not doing what they already know they should do that companies get into trouble over quality."
>
> Philip B. Crosby
> *Quality Without Tears*

Ethic 9

The Sustainability Ethic

It is ethical to consider the long-range implications of your decision-making and to make sustainability a guiding tenet. It is unethical to knowingly implement practices that ensure the collapse or diminished health of self, organization, or environment.

Restatement of Ethic 9:

It is ethical to submit all personal, organizational, cultural, and environmental practices to close scrutiny, altering them until they are as sustainable and free of traps as possible. It is unethical to knowingly implement practices that ensure environmental collapse, and unethical, as well, to implement practices that diminish the health and wellbeing of individuals.

Personal Traps are where the individual engages in behavior that has immediate or short term advantages but long term disadvantages.

Organizational Traps are where the individual engages in behavior that has immediate or short-term advantages for the individual engaging in the behavior but immediate or long-term disadvantages for the organization.

Personal Fences, on the other hand, are where the individual engages in behavior that has immediate or short-term disadvantages but long term advantages.

Organizational Fence is a situation in which behavior has immediate or short-term disadvantages for the individual who engages in it but immediate or long-term advantages for the organization.

John R. Platt[SEP]
"Social Traps"

Ethic 10

The Wind Harp Ethic

It is ethical to treat others in and out of the organization as you would like to be treated even though you are not always so treated. It is unethical not to find appropriate avenues for the release of your anger, resentment, and rage. It is unethical to engage in scapegoating.

Restatement of Ethic 10:

It is ethical to treat others in and out of the organization as you would like to be treated even though you are not always so treated. It is unethical not to find appropriate avenues for the release of your anger, resentment and rage so as to keep from passing them on to, or taking them out on others. It is unethical to engage in scapegoating.

"The way employees treat customers reflects the manner in which they're being treated by management."

>James A. Perkins -- Federal Express, quoted in *The Healthy Company* by Robert H. Rosen

"Treat them all in a lofty manner lest they have cause to find thee weak."

>John Dee
>18th century metaphysician

Ethic 11

The Personal Growth Ethic

It is ethical to continue to grow as a person, to continue to increase your capacity to conduct yourself in accord with your ethics and principles. It is unethical to stop growing as a person.

Restatement of Ethic 11:

It is ethical to continue to grow as a person, to continue to increase your capacity to conduct yourself in accord with your ethics and principles. It is unethical not to continue the life-long process of personal/psychological development.

> *"The measure of individuals--and so of corporations--is the extent to which we struggle to complete ourselves, the energy we devote to living up to our potential."*
>
> Max De Pree
> *Leadership is an Art*

> *"No organization can be more progressive or more effective than its people."*
>
> Henry Ford II
> *The Human Environment and Business*

Ethic 12

The Gift-Sharing Ethic

It is ethical to utilize your gifts, talents, and unique experience on behalf of your organization. It is unethical not to share your gifts, talents, and unique experience somewhere, for the benefit of someone.

Restatement of Ethic 12:

It is ethical to utilize your gifts, talents, and unique experience on behalf of your organization. Through the expression of your unique gifts you may help your organization evolve and in the process acquire for yourself a greater sense of purpose and meaning. It is unethical not to share your gifts, talents, and unique experience somewhere, for the benefit of someone; and your organization does represent one place, if not the only place, where sharing your gifts can benefit others.

> *"You can assume that you are fulfilling your purpose if you are in the process of turning your experience into products and events that bring advantage to others."*
>
> Buckminster Fuller
> Inventor, poet, philosopher

References & Notes

The work of innumerable writers, thinkers, philosophers and others from a variety of disciplines have been consulted and drawn on in the development of the ethics of human development. For the purposes of this book, I want to acknowledge ethicist John David Garcia whose work directly influenced ethics 2, 3, 4, 7 and 12. Buckminster Fuller's work directly influenced ethics 5 and 12. For a more extensive crediting of references as well as a more complete explanation of each ethic, see *Human Logic and the Theater of Everyday Life* and *Right Livelihood: The Twelve Ethics of Work*, both by David Thomas, PhD.

Ethics defined: "the study of standards of conduct"-- Webster's New World Dictionary, Second Edition; to the question, *"How ought I to behave?"* the philosopher Immanuel Kant wrote, *"Ethics provides the answer."*

FINAL NOTE: "No matter how complete and thorough the recommended code of conduct (for example, this code: *The Ethics of Human Development*), there will be moments that call for totally unique responses, responses different and more "ethical" than those prescribed by the code. When that happens, your obligation is to the moment and not to the code. *"Be it how it will, do right now," is* the way Emerson put it, even if it means abandoning the code. The expert chef follows the recipe to a "T" until knowledge or intuition tells him or her that by varying the recipe, he or she can produce a more perfect dish. There will be exceptions to the ethics of human development but in general—when in doubt—they prescribe the safest direction in which to err."

David Thomas, PhD
Human Logic and the Theater of Everyday Life

The *Quick Guide* can be ordered through area booksellers. For more information on *The Ethics of Human Development Training Program*, go to: *davidthomasphd.com, or* contact David Thomas, PhD: dtec@cox.net.

Other Ethics of Human Development books:

Human Logic and the Theater of Everyday Life

Right Livelihood: The Twelve Ethics of Work

The Ethics of Human Development Training Program: Complete Guide

The Ethics of Human Development Workbook

Available through area booksellers.